A BOUQUET FROM THE KITCHEN

To _____

From _____

The discovery of a new dish does more for the happiness of mankind than the discovery of a star.

BRILLAT-SAVARIN

A BOUQUET from the KITCHEN

*A special collection of recipes,
kitchen wisdom and lore*

by Jane Parker Resnick

LONGMEADOW PRESS

A BOUQUET FROM THE KITCHEN

Text copyright © 1991 by Jane Parker Resnick

Design copyright © 1991 by Longmeadow Press

Published by Longmeadow Press, 201 High Ridge Road, Stamford, Connecticut 06904. No part of this book may be reproduced or used in any form or by any means, electronic or mechanical, including photocopying, recording or by any information storage and retrieval system, without permission in writing from the publisher.

ISBN: 0-681-41124-4

Printed in Singapore

0 9 8 7 6 5 4 3 2 1

Jacket and interior design by Lisa Amoroso

The Victorian patterns used on the section openings of this book are from the fabric and wallpaper collections of Brunschwig & Fils, Inc., and are reproduced by their kind permission. The publisher gratefully acknowledges the assistance of Mrs. Murray Douglas and Judy Straeten in the preparation of this book.

CONTENTS

A Cookie Jar of Memories

The Bountiful Bread Basket

The Charms of Chocolate

The Comforts of Home

The Gracious Hostess

The Scent of Spice

Bright Beginnings

Classic Conclusions

INTRODUCTION

This book is meant as a gift for anyone who reads it, but I know that with each person who does, I will receive much more in return. It sounds a note for the great pleasure in preparing foods reminiscent of childhood and comfort and indulgence. Too often, we forget. More often, we are too busy. But if one of these recipes, or one of my thoughts, inspires the baking of a good bread, the making of a hearty soup, I know that the cook and her family and friends will be well rewarded. And I will be, too.

Part of the fun in writing this book has been in thinking about the everyday but meaningful ways women create a sense of home and ease for the people they love. The women who, over the years, have shared these recipes with me are part of the chain of receiving by giving that I hope you will enjoy when you give this book to someone else.

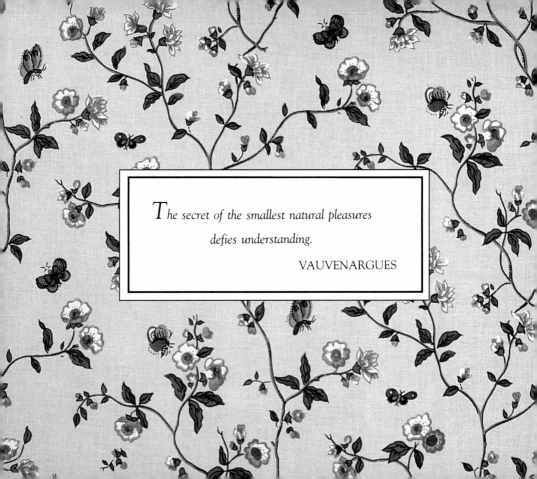

*The secret of the smallest natural pleasures
defies understanding.*

VAUVENARGUES

A
Cookie Jar of
Memories

A taste of a scallop shaped cookie called a Madeleine evoked the childhood memories that inspired Marcel Proust to write his masterpiece, *Remembrance of Things Past.* To Proust, who had eaten Madeleines in his childhood, they carried, "in the tiny and almost impalpable drop of their essence, the vast structure of recollection."

Cookies are like that. Memories cling to them, not just in their taste and fragrance, but in their making. All children love to make cookies, and if we stop making them as adults, we lose some of the child within us. Cookies create good memories, and both are meant to be shared.

Unexpected guests are part of life's unpredictability, but with homemade cookies on hand you are always prepared. A batch of dough in the freezer, ready to be sliced and popped into the oven, and homemade cookies are only minutes away. Welcome guests with them, rush them over to an unhappy friend, or send them to school with a child. You'll never be caught without a cookie.

TENDERHEARTED COOKIES

1 ½ cups all-purpose flour

½ teaspoon baking soda

¾ teaspoon salt

½ cup butter or margarine

½ cup sugar

½ cup brown sugar

1 egg

2 teaspoons vanilla

½ cup chopped nuts

Combine flour, baking soda, and salt. Mix butter, sugar, egg and vanilla until fluffy. Gradually mix in flour and nuts. Turn dough onto counter and shape into roll, 1 ½" in diameter. Wrap and refrigerate or freeze. When ready to bake, heat oven to 375°. Slice dough at ⅛" to ¼" intervals. Cut the whole roll or as many as needed and return rest to refrigerator. Place on ungreased cookie sheet and bake 10 minutes.

For chocolate cookies, add 3 squares of melted unsweetened chocolate to the egg mixture and eliminate 1 teaspoon of vanilla.

'Tis an ill cook that cannot lick his own fingers.

WILLIAM SHAKESPEARE

It is a true expression of character to resist a cookie right from the oven.

The love of making them and the love of sharing them makes cookies the most affectionate of all foods.

Maintaining the proper texture of cookies while storing them can be tricky. For the right crunch, follow these general rules:

Store crisp cookies in a loosely sealed container. If they soften, they can be recrisped on a baking sheet in a low oven for five minutes.

Store soft cookies in a tightly sealed container. If they become dry, they will regain moisture if a piece of apple is added to the container.

Cookies that have cooled too long on the cookie sheet can become stuck. To loosen, put them back in the oven for a minute or two or run the sheet over a burner to warm the bottom.

*T*hat man is richest whose pleasures are

the cheapest.

HENRY DAVID THOREAU

The
Bountiful Bread
Basket

Since ancient times, bread has had spiritual significance as a symbol of life and thankfulness. Even today, breadmaking retains an aura of the mysterious and miraculous, connecting us to the past through timeless tactile sensations and the deep satisfaction that has always been the fruit of earnest, gentle labor. To make bread now is to know the same pleasure that every cook has ever known when taking this most creative and essential food from the oven.

The beauty of yeast is its flexibility and, at times, its unpredictability. So with a little practice and experimentation, the breadmaking process can fit anyone's schedule. A lifetime of rewards will follow the effort, for there is no aroma equal to the smell of baking bread and few greater pleasures than bringing a freshly baked loaf to the table.

HEAVENLY WHITE BREAD

1 package active dry yeast

2 cups warm milk (approx. 100° to 115°)

2 tablespoons sugar

¼ cup melted butter

1 tablespoon salt

5 to 6 cups all-purpose flour

Add yeast and sugar to ½ cup of the warm milk. Stir until dissolved and small bubbles will appear on the surface. Place the remaining milk, butter and salt in a bowl and stir in 3 cups of flour, one at a time, mixing well. Add the yeast mixture, then continue to add flour and stir until the mixture is somewhat firm.

Scrape the dough onto a floured surface and let it rest for a moment. Knead for 10 minutes, adding flour to keep it from sticking. When the dough is smooth and elastic, place in a large buttered bowl. Turn the dough to butter all sides, and cover with a towel. Let rise until double in volume (an hour or two).

Turn the dough onto a floured surface, punch down, knead for 5 minutes, and cut in half with a sharp knife. Shape into two loaves and place into well-buttered 9 inch loaf pans. Cover with a towel and let rise until almost double in volume (about an hour).

Brush the tops with water and bake in a preheated 400° oven for 40 to 45 minutes or until the bread sounds hollow when tapped. Remove from pans and cool on a rack.

One hallmark of a good bread is its crust. And while every step is important to the breadmaking process, a small but crowning touch can make the difference.

To encourage a crust to harden, brush the dough with an egg white beaten with a tablespoon of water before placing in the oven.

To soften a crust, brush the loaf with melted butter as it emerges from the oven. Or cover with a towel as it cools on a rack.

If a very hard crust is a problem, place a small pan of water in the oven with the baking bread.

To keep the bottom and sides from becoming soggy, always remove the bread from the pan and cool on a rack.

I never had a piece of toast
Particularly long and wide,
But fell upon the sanded floor,
And always on the buttered side.

JAMES PAYN

And the best bread was of
my mother's own making—
the best in all the land!

HENRY JAMES

Acorns were good until bread was found.   FRANCIS BACON

Bread deals with living things, with giving life, with growth, with the seed, the grain that
nurtures. It is no coincidence that we say bread is the staff of life.

LIONEL POILANE

If seduction is a sin, chocolate is guilty.

The
Charms of
Chocolate

A drink, frothy, intoxicating, first appeared in the courts of Europe in the 16th century. Mornings, the aristocracy indulged in this creation in bed . . . served in Chinese porcelain cups on golden saucers. The drink was chocolate.

To courtiers, chocolate became a symbol of sophistication, colored ever so deliciously with the erotic and decadent. Chocolate was part of *l'amour*, and love, then as now, was the passion of life.

Two hundred years later, when chocolate became a confection, chocolatiers transformed the original drink into a far more voluptuous experience—chocolate with a sensual silkiness that melts, slowly in the mouth. Today, it has lost none of its appeal.

A whole pot of homemade hot fudge sauce is the most delicious of indulgences. This recipe is potently chocolate but not excessively sweet. It keeps wonderfully in the refrigerator for several weeks and is a truly surprising treat for unexpected guests. Always serve an abundance of hot fudge on sundaes. No one dares to admit to the amount they *really* want, but everyone is delighted to be spoiled.

RICH FUDGE SAUCE

1 can evaporated milk, 12 oz.
1¾ cups sugar
4 ounces unsweetened chocolate
  (broken into pieces)

¼ cup butter or margarine
1 teaspoon vanilla
½ teaspoon salt

Heat milk and sugar to rolling boil, stirring constantly. Boil and stir 1 minute. Add chocolate and stir until melted. Beat over heat until smooth. (If slightly curdled in appearance, beat vigorously until creamy.) Remove from heat and blend in butter, vanilla and salt.

Oh, *but it seems no chocolate chip cookie ever has enough chocolate chips.*

A *craving for chocolate is a lust for life.*

E*ating chocolate is like love. It should be entered into with abandon or not at all.*

P*eople give chocolate to say "I'm sorry," "I love you," "thank you," "I'm thinking of you." Chocolate speaks the language of the emotions.*

I*t has been shown as proof positive that carefully prepared chocolate is as healthful a food as it is pleasant; that it is nourishing and easily digested . . . (and) that it is above all helpful to people who must do a great deal of mental work.*

JEAN-ANTHELME BRILLAT-SAVARIN

Chocolate can be temperamental when melting and stiffen seemingly on a whim. For the best results, chop chocolate into pieces and begin with a perfectly dry pan. Melt in the top pan of a double boiler over hot, not boiling, water. Or heat two or three inches of water in a frying pan, remove from the heat and place a small covered pan containing the chocolate in the water. In 5 minutes, the chocolate should be melted. If not, reheat the water.

—If chocolate does stiffen, all is not lost. Beat in a little water or melted shortening until it smooths out.

❧

When the cupboard is bare of what the recipe calls for, there are ready substitutions for chocolates—

❧

Bittersweet chocolate can be substituted for semisweet at any time with only a slight change in flavor. One ounce (1 square) of unsweetened chocolate equals 3 tablespoons of cocoa plus 1 tablespoon of shortening or margarine.

❧

A half cup of semi-sweet pieces for melting is interchangeable with 3 ounces of semi-sweet chocolate.

*H*ome is not where you live but where

they understand you.

CHRISTIAN MORGENSTERN

The
Comforts of
Home

A home is like a pot of soup kept simmering on the stove. An embracing warmth is in that pot, and nourishment, too, for both the body and the spirit. Like a good bowl of soup, a home is much more than the sum of its parts, for the qualities of comfort and sustenance are in the blending, not in the individual ingredients. Creating a home is more than supplying shelter. It requires work, patience, and an understanding that providing comfort for oneself and others is a joyous effort.

It is difficult to finish a bowl of chicken soup without a feeling of well-being. Whether credence is given to chicken soup's curative powers or not, a bowl of chicken soup certainly *feels* good. A basic food in every sense, chicken soup can still be as idiosyncratic as the cook. Chicken, onions, carrots, celery and parsnips suffice for some, but others may add noodles, rice, vegetables, whatever gives chicken soup the special comforting quality it has in every home.

—— GREAT AUNT LENA'S CHICKEN SOUP ——

1 chicken (4 to 5 pounds) or chicken parts

3 quarts water

1 tablespoon salt

1 large yellow onion

3 ribs of celery with leafy tops

3 carrots, peeled

3 parsnips, peeled

Salt and pepper to taste

Rinse the chicken and trim off excess fat. If whole, cut the chicken into quarters and place in large stock pot. Add water and salt. Cover and heat to boiling. Skim off scum from the top.

Add onions and celery. Simmer covered for 1 hour.

Cut the carrots and parsnips in half, add to stock and simmer until tender—about 1 hour.

Remove the chicken and vegetables and reserve.

Strain the stock. At this point, the soup can be frozen and used whenever chicken stock is called for.

Cut the reserved carrots and parsnips into strips. A few minutes before serving, add the vegetables, adjust seasoning, heat and serve.

Cold salted water is the best soup starter because it coaxes the most flavor from the ingredients.

To avoid overcooking or curdling soup, be sure to add ingredients in the order specified by a recipe. To keep milk from curdling when adding to hot soup, add the soup to the milk rather than the milk to the soup.

Soup too salty? Place raw potato slices in the soup and boil for a short time.

Soup too thin? Add mashed potatoes or pureed cooked vegetables to give soup body and flavor.

Garnishes for soups can enhance their taste and texture. Try these: croutons, popcorn, chopped nuts, grated cheese, diced vegetables, or crumbled bacon.

Home was quite a place when people stayed there.   E.B. WHITE

Home is the place where,
When you have to go there,
They have to take you in.

ROBERT FROST

Home is where the heart is.   PLINY THE ELDER

We need not power or splendor,
Wide Hall or lordly dome;
The good, the true, the tender,
These form the wealth of home.

SARAH JOSEPH HALE

Home interprets Heaven. Home is heaven for beginners.   CHARLES PARKHURST

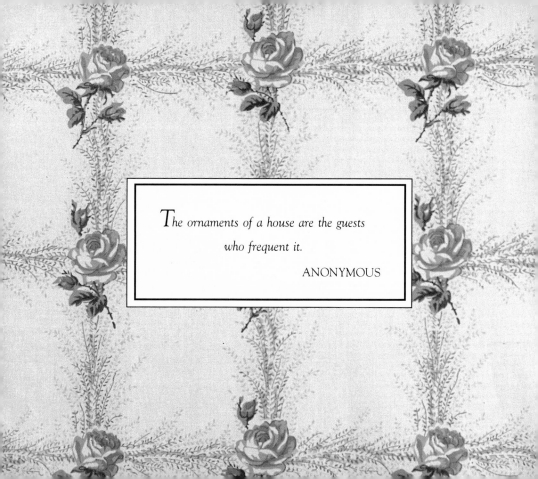

The ornaments of a house are the guests
who frequent it.

ANONYMOUS

The
Gracious
Hostess

Greeting guests with generosity and graciousness is not an art, but an instinct. Every hostess wants her home to be welcoming and her guests to be comfortable. And the more relaxed the hostess appears, the happier her guests are going to be. So the fuss over details, linens and soap, silverware and supper, is necessarily a backstage event. The wise hostess knows that the goal of entertaining, pampering and indulging her guests is that, ultimately, they feel quite simply at home.

The beauty of this cake is its flexibility. Moist, rich, yet not too sweet, this delicious creation enhances any meal from morning till midnight. At brunch or lunch this cake is dessert with just a kiss of sweetness. A thick slice with coffee or tea is substantial and satisfying. Dinner guests will adore it and, with a glass of milk, late night snackers will find it an irresistible way to end the day.

A MOST CONGENIAL COFFEE CAKE

BATTER:

2 sticks unsalted butter

2 cups sugar

2 eggs, beaten

2 cups all-purpose flour

1 tablespoon baking powder

¼ teaspoon salt

2 cups sour cream

1 tablespoon vanilla

TOPPING:

¾ cup sugar

2 cups pecans, chopped

1 tablespoon cinnamon

Preheat oven to 350°. Grease and lightly flour a 10″ bundt pan. Mix together flour, baking powder and salt. Combine ¾ cup sugar, pecans and cinnamon in another bowl.

Cream butter and sugar; add eggs, blending well. Mix in sour cream and vanilla. Fold in the dry ingredients and beat until just blended. Pour half the batter into the pan and sprinkle with half the topping. Add the rest of the batter and top with the remaining pecan/sugar mixture. Bake for 60 minutes or until a tester inserted in the center comes out clean. Serves 10.

Hospitality consists in a little fire, a little food, and an immense quiet.

RALPH WALDO EMERSON

There is an emanation from the heart in genuine hospitality which cannot be described but is immediately felt, and puts the stranger at once at his ease.

WASHINGTON IRVING

The hostess must be like the duck– calm and unruffled on the surface and paddling like mad underneath.

ANONYMOUS

Some people can stay longer in an hour than others can in a week.

W.D. HOWELLS

To invite a person into your house is to take charge of his happiness for as long as he is under your roof.

BRILLAT-SAVARIN

For best cake results, preheat the oven for 15 minutes and check for doneness a few minutes before the recommended time.

❦

Bake a cake as soon as possible after the batter is mixed or it will become heavy.

❦

Line the bottom of a pan with waxed paper and the cake will never stick.

❦

To keep nuts and raisins from sinking in a cake, coat them with flour. Always add them to the batter at the end of the mixing.

❦

No toothpicks? Use a piece of spaghetti to test a cake for doneness.

❦

When transferring a cake to a plate, put sugar on the plate first. The sugar will absorb moisture and the bottom of the cake will never become soggy or stick to the plate.

*S*pices are. . . . *"the hidden soul of cooking."*

GRINOD DE LA REYNIERE
the father of French cuisine

The
Scent of Spice

The scent of herbs and spices, sweet and sharp, pungent and mild, are the spirit of the kitchen. To season food is to move from merely cooking to creating, from providing sustenance to feeding the soul. The addition of a single spice can make ordinary food interesting and a blending of herbs and spices can transform simple food into an indefinable eating experience. Spices have two inseparable qualities, taste and aroma, which combine almost magically to create much of our enjoyment of food.

Cinnamon is one of the oldest spices known to man. Even though it is found in both sweet and savory dishes throughout the world, we tend to regard this spice as the fragrance of beloved desserts. Indeed, combined with nutmeg and cloves, cinnamon is the perfume of this "spice" cake. A dense, moist confection, this cake has emerged from ovens for generations not only because it is delicious and satisfying, but because it *smells* so good.

SUMPTUOUS SPICE CAKE

1¾ cups flour

¼ teaspoon salt

1 teaspoon baking soda

1 teaspoon cinnamon

½ teaspoon nutmeg

½ teaspoon ground cloves

½ cup (1 stick) butter

1½ cups brown sugar, firmly packed

2 eggs, well beaten

1 cup sour cream

1 cup raisins

½ cup chopped walnuts

Preheat oven to 350°. Lightly grease a 9x5x3 inch loaf pan.

Combine flour, salt, soda and spices; set aside.

Cream butter, adding sugar gradually and blending well. Add eggs and mix. Stir in dry ingredients alternately with sour cream. Add raisins and nuts. Pour the batter into pan and bake 45 to 50 minutes. When cool, sprinkle with confectioner's sugar.

Dried herbs and spices are more pungent than fresh, so increase the quantity when using fresh herbs. As a general rule, use 1 tablespoon of a fresh herb when a recipe calls for 1 teaspoon dried or ¼ teaspoon ground or powdered herb.

Release the bouquet of dried herbs and spices by crushing them in the palm of your hand before adding them to food.

Dried herbs and spices, like youth and fair weather, don't last forever. Open the bottles and sniff now and then to test for strength. A spice that has lost its aroma is just cluttering the cupboard.

For a change of flavor in your favorite foods, add a pinch of: thyme to carrots; mint to peas; basil to tomatoes; dill to potatoes; sage to chicken; oregano to eggs.

And Hezekiah hearkened unto them and showed them all the house of his precious things, the silver and the gold and the spice.   2 KINGS 20:13

As aromatic plants bestow
No spicy fragrance while they grow,
But crushed or trodden to the ground
Diffuse their balmy sweets around.

OLIVER GOLDSMITH

*B*reakfast is the forecast of the whole day.

LEIGH HUNT

Bright
Beginnings

 *good* breakfast, a meal that soothes and fortifies, cheers and satisfies, is a joy. Breakfast fills the morning's hungry desire and fuels both the body and the spirit. It is an opportunity to choose foods that feel good, foods that are both sensible and indulgent, like a bowl of nourishing hot cereal, a thickly cut slice of wholesome bread, or a perfect soft-boiled egg. There is no more personal meal than breakfast, so let desire dictate. Gratification at breakfast is a fitting beginning for every day.

Pancakes are reminiscent of late-starting days that never wander far from the kitchen. A seductive cross between a meal and a dessert, pancakes are substantial enough to be satisfying and still sweet enough to be frivolous. This time-tested recipe can only be improved upon with personal additions: fruit or nuts or whatever makes breakfast the bright beginning it should be.

___ COUNTRY PANCAKES WITH HOT BLUEBERRY SAUCE ___

2 eggs, beaten	1¼ cups all-purpose flour	4 teaspoons baking powder
4 tablespoons butter, melted	1 tablespoon sugar	¾ teaspoon salt
1 cup milk		

In one bowl, stir the butter into the milk; add the eggs and mix well. In another bowl, combine the flour, sugar, baking powder and salt. Pour the egg mixture into the flour mixture and stir until the dry ingredients are well moistened. Do not overmix.

Heat a griddle or skillet, grease lightly, and drop 2 or 3 tablespoons of batter for each pancake. When bubbles break on the surface, turn and cook until the bottom is lightly browned. Makes 2 dozen 4-inch pancakes.

_____ BLUEBERRY SAUCE _____

1½ cups fresh blueberries	½ teaspoon cinnamon	grated lemon rind
¼ cup sugar	¼ teaspoon nutmeg	

Mix blueberries with remaining ingredients in a saucepan. Bring to a boil and simmer for 5 minutes, stirring occasionally. Serve hot over pancakes.

Breakfast makes a good memory. RABELAIS

Nothing helps the scenery like ham and eggs.

MARK TWAIN

Life within doors has few pleasanter prospects than a neatly arranged and well-provisioned breakfast table.

NATHANIEL HAWTHORNE

The breakfast table is not a bulletin board for the curing of horrible dreams and depressing symptoms, but the place where a bright keynote for the day is struck.

PROF. B.G. JEFFRIES, M.S., FAMILY RECEIPTS:
The Household Guide or Domestic Cyclopedia (1902)

The critical period in matrimony is breakfast-time. A.P. HERBERT

Pancake batter can be kept in the refrigerator for a few days. If it thickens, you can thin it by adding milk a tablespoon at a time.

❧

Create especially tender pancakes by making the batter the night before, omitting the baking powder and adding it in the morning.

❧

Avoid turning a pancake more than once—it will toughen.

❧

To keep pancakes warm before serving, place them in a low oven between folds of a kitchen towel.

The daintiest last, to make the end most sweet.

WILLIAM SHAKESPEARE

Classic
Conclusions

Dessert, served as it is at the very end of the meal, is not the object of hunger, but of desire. And how sweet it is! Nothing pleases or satisfies like dessert; nothing is more anticipated or remains longer in the memory than a glorious dessert. Outstanding desserts never go unnoticed, for everyone appreciates the singular sweet moment when dinner ends splendidly with a memorable, classic conclusion.

_____ A GRAND SOUFFLE AU GRAND MARNIER _____

Base:

3 tablespoons flour

¼ cup milk

⅓ cup sugar

3 tablespoons orange marmalade

4 egg yolks

3 tablespoons Grand Marnier

2 teaspoons vanilla

Egg Whites:

5 egg whites, at room temperature

Pinch of salt

2 tablespoons sugar

Preheat oven to 375°. Butter a 1½ quart souffle or straight-sided baking dish and sprinkle sugar over the sides and bottom. Add a "collar" of 2 or 3 inches of foil, secured with straight pins, to allow the souffle to rise above the edge of the dish. Butter the collar before attaching.

Base: Whisk the flour and half of the milk into a sauce pan to blend. Beat in the rest of the milk and sugar. Add the marmalade. Stir over medium heat until the mixture thickens. Whisk briefly as it comes to a boil. It will be very thick. Remove from heat, let cool for a moment, then beat in egg yolks one at a time.

Egg Whites: Beat the egg whites until foaming; add salt and beat to soft peaks. Add sugar and beat to soft, shining peaks.

To combine: Beat Grand Marnier and vanilla into the base. Stir ¼ of the egg whites into the mixture. Then rapidly fold in the remaining egg whites and turn souffle into the dish.

Note: The souffle may be completed to this point ½ hour or more ahead. Cover loosely with foil.

Bake 30 minutes or until puffed and lightly browned. Serves 4.

Egg whites must be at room temperature to beat well. You can hasten the process by placing whole eggs in warm water for 10 minutes or setting the mixing bowl of whites in a larger bowl of warm water for a few minutes.

Egg whites will not whip if they contain ANY yolk. To retrieve even the smallest bit of yolk from whites, scoop it out with a piece of egg shell. To avoid problems, separate each egg white into a cup before adding to the others in case the yolk is broken.

The bowl for beating egg whites must be impeccably dry and clean, free of oil or grease.

Begin beating egg whites at a moderate speed until they are foaming. Then add a pinch of salt and, for 4 egg whites, ¼ teaspoon of cream of tartar to act as stabilizers. Gradually increase speed to fast.

An apple pie without some cheese is like a kiss without a squeeze.

ENGLISH RHYME

After a good dinner, one can forgive anybody,
even one's own relations.

OSCAR WILDE

A man cannot have a pure mind who
refuses apple dumplings.

CHARLES LAMB

Who wants some pudding nice and hot!
  'Tis now the time to try it.
Just taken from the smoking pot,
  And taste before you buy it.

OLD LONDON STREET CRY

ABOUT THE AUTHOR

Jane Parker Resnick is a gifted writer and restaurant critic who has many articles and books to her credit including the bestselling *The Souffle Also Rises* and *A Friend Makes All The Difference*. Known to her friends and family as a cook extraordinaire, Jane is also an avid outdoors enthusiast who enjoys canoeing, rafting, fishing and skiing with her family. She lives with her husband and daughter by a lake in rural Connecticut.

ABOUT THE DESIGNER

Lisa Amoroso is a talented artist and in-house jacket designer for a major New York publisher. A graduate of the Parson School of Design, she has always loved to draw and paint and has illustrated several children's books. She lives in New York City with her husband, John, and her two birds, Avalon and Lettle.